Visions of Life

Poems and Prose Inspired by the Vicious Cycle of Our Lives

Visions of Life

Poems and Prose Inspired by the Vicious Cycle of Our Lives

Helen T. Jeffries

Copyright © 2022. Helen T. Jeffries. All rights reserved.

This book or any portion thereof may not be reproduced or used in any manner whatsoever without the express written permission of the publisher and author except for the use of brief quotations in a book review.

Printed in the United States of America

First Printing, 2022

ISBN: 978-1-951883-86-7

The Butterfly Typeface Publishing
PO Box 56193
Little Rock AR 72215

www.thebutterflytypeface.com

Dedication

These poems are dedicated to my parents, Andrew and Helen Williams Jeffries. Without you, there would be no me. Your words of wisdom and encouragement will forever linger in my soul.

Your baby girl,

Helen Teryce "Teri" Jeffries

"What life has in store for us can sometimes be an awakening to our world."

-Helen T. Jeffries

Table Of Contents

PICK UP THE PIECES 23

BROKEN UNITY 24

JELLY 26

SHIP OF ZION 27

LEARN TO BE YOURSELF 28

SITTING IN THE PARK 30

GRAY EYES 31

THE LOVE EXPERIENCE 33

T.V. SOAP STORY 34

THE HURTING TRUTH 35

WHO'S THAT LADY? 36

MAN'S HELPER 37

DANCING IN THE STREET 38

THINKING 39

MR. WINTER	41
MISPLACED	42
MISTREATMENT	43
GOING FORWARD	44
HEY LOVE	45
SNEAKY PEOPLE	47
ANYONE	48
DISCIPLINE	50
SPIRITUAL BEING	53
MONTHS OF THE YEAR	54
LONELINESS REPLACED	55
A DAUGHTER'S LOVE	56
THE RESPONSIBILITY of FAME	57
THE WORKPLACE	59
MY GUY	61

THE FOUR SEASONS	62
PEOPLE AND ISSUES	64
OH, CHILD	66
HISTORY OF EQUALITY	67
A DATE WITH JENNY	69
CLASSROOM MEMORIES	71
SCHOOL RULES	72
SIDE SHOW EVENT	75
PLANTING A SEED	77
LIFE	79
CHANGE	80
A NEW WORLD	81
CRUISING TOGETHER	85
KNOWING MY SAVIOUR	87
LESSONS OF LIFE	88

THE ROAD TO SUCCESS	90
RISEN	92
EASTER CELEBRATION	95
A MIGHTY LOVE	96
LONELY NIGHT	97
THE TUB	99
DINNER TROUBLE	101
OBSERVING REALITY	104
A FAMILY OF NINE	105
SADDEN THOUGHTS	107
PICNIC FUN	108
SPRING SEASON	109
EXPRESSIONS OF SORROW	110
MONEY	111
PRECIOUS GEM	112

THE ONE I LOVE	113
FUN ON THE BEACH	115
CHECKING IT OUT	116
FEAR TO HOPE	118
CHILDHOOD SWEETHEART	120
TAKE IT AS IT COMES	123
THE FEEL OF INSTRUMENTS I LOVE	124
THE VOYAGE OF TIME	125
OH, YE OF LITTLE FAITH	129
ENCOURAGEMENT	131
VAN RIDE	132
MOTHER'S GIFT FROM GOD	133
TO A PHENOMENAL MOTHER	134
SUCCESS	136
BECOMING A YOUNG ADULT	137

MOTHER'S SPIRITUAL GUIDANCE 138

BITTERNESS WITHOUT A CAUSE 140

BEING AN EXAMPLE 142

FULFILING OUR LIVES 144

VIOLENCE 145

PROBLEMS 146

AUTHORITY 148

THE CONTROL FACTOR 150

ANGER 151

EXAMPLES DADS POSSESS 153

SPIRITUAL AND EARTHLY FATHERS 155

LIFE CHALLENGES 157

MANKIND 158

CONCLUSION 161

About the Author 163

Foreword

There were six active siblings in the Jeffries home when in 1961, number seven arrived. The years between us ranged from 7 to 20, so we marveled at this baby's presence. I had prayed for a little sister and appointed myself the primary keeper of this little one. Her name was "Helen Teryce Jeffries."

Mom and Dad made our home a warm, loving, and welcoming environment. There were always delicious homemade desserts on the dining room table daily available to our friends and us. There were also edible leftovers in the fridge at one's fingertips.

"Teri," as we affectionately called her, was a sweet, bright spirit of a being who loved God, her family, friends, reading and writing. She inspired our parents to order the complete series of the "My Book House" library. These books began with Nursery Rhymes, Fiction and Non-Fiction stories, and continued with Biographies and Auto-Biographies of famous people. These books and their content were visited by her and mom at least once a day, weekly for years. Teri could repeat them verbatim if you said the titles.

Teri has many skills and gifts, but the one that seems to bring her the most joy is writing and sharing her words with others.

Challenged with an Epileptic Disorder, Teri resided in the family home for more than forty-nine years. Within that period, our father, Andrew Jeffries, passed in December of 2003. Our mom, Helen Juanita Jeffries, passed in May of 2010. One month after our mom's demise, Teri was lonely, sad, and virtually depressed.

She proceeded to experience the influence of our mom's sweet spirit late at night in the house. One night, it was not a fearful emotion that covered her heart and mind, but a clear and urgent message "Start Writing Poems!" Teri arose the following day, and throughout the days and nights to come, she would write!

For the next two years, she wrote profusely - over one-hundred and twenty poems - one after another.

Writing is not only her ministry. It is her Medicine.

Despite an epileptic disorder, Teri took to the pen to see her way through gaps in verbal communication, using it as medicine to keep her brain sharpened and her hands steady enough to do something creative that is uniquely hers.

You are about to enter an amazing world of divine, engaging, imaginable, and relatable poetry.

Enjoy the Journey. I Did!

Belynda Joyce Jeffries,

Sister

Acknowledgments

First, I give honor and glory to God who never missed a beat in supplying all my needs when I felt down and out. I am truly blessed.

Kudos to my sorors and friends who put up with listening to my poetry and giving their opinions, even if it was late at night. Blessings to those who rooted me on to the finish line.

Lastly, thanks to my sister, Belynda, for helping and encouraging me to take it to the next level.

Also, Chrishna, without you this would not be happening. Thanks for your input that helped make this collection a reality.

To my church, New Millennium, and its members, along with the church of my youth, Mt. Pleasant Baptist Church, whose ideals, and examples directed my path to a spiritual growth of understanding and love.

Introduction

After my mother's demise in 2010, it was as though her lingering spirit, in our home took over. I was compelled with an intense desire to write poetry and prose.

Having lived in our home with my mother for 53 years, I had the privilege of observing many activities others may consider mundane in ways that were anything but ordinary from my perspective.

The wet and dry humor of my parents, the book and street sense supplied by my siblings, and my unique point of view all worked together to create this tapestry of love and life.

In writing this book, I discovered feelings of hope, sadness, happiness, and a faith grounded in a connection with God.

It is my hope that as you read your heart will be touched spiritually, physically, and emotionally.

So, if you're ready to explore your mind, come go with me.

PICK UP THE PIECES

Never had to be without food, shelter,
or love.
And I am grateful to the Father above.

My life has been calm, sometimes stormy
by the raging foamy sea.
Yet, as time goes on, I say to myself,
"The Lord is blessing me."

Life goes in a circle, sometimes in a triangle
and sometimes in a square.
But eventually I know
that I will definitely get there.

The crooked can be made straight
and the rough places ironed out.
Then I'm on easy street - dancing about.

Hang on in there babe.
You'll get there soon enough.
I tell others, "I sure will.
I'm going to hang tough!"

BROKEN UNITY

Where is the love that we always shared?
It disappeared like a ghost into the morning air.

It was unreal. The love chain was broken,
and coming apart at the seams.
All that was comfortable was left in a dream.

Memories of happiness, laughter, and joy,
were left behind -
leaving a family angry and quite annoyed.

I know. It happened right before my eyes.
I didn't understand why
some members were despised.

Could it be envy, madness, lies, or greed?
I don't understand why
one would plant that seed.

Why couldn't we be thankful
for those who worked so hard?
Instead, we are suspicious,
and stay on guard.

Lord, we have strayed from the glories of love,
given to us by the father above.

Some siblings went east, the others west,
not realizing that together
they can give their best.

Be careful in saying who's wrong.
Instead, think of a way to get along.

Put your eyes on a bigger prize.
Be happy.
Get together.
Apologize.

JELLY

Here I go again, falling in love once more.
Here I go again, listening for words to store.

I took the words spoken to my heart,
knowing from the very start,
But the words he said I adored.

I tried to be mean and spite,
Saying he didn't do me right,

But the words he said to me made me
drop to my knees.
I couldn't even fight.

I am walking toward my house to get the mail,
wishing he would go to hell.

But he runs to my side saying,
"Baby, let's take a ride."
I'm in his car sitting for a spell.

SHIP OF ZION

Tis the old ship of Zion!
Everybody get on board!
There is room for all people.
Happiness galore.

Some are dancing, others shouting,
feeling the joy of peace.
Others sitting down to enjoy a great feast.

We will tell stories about prophets
and the ancestors of old-
how they showed no fear but were very bold.

Tell all the folks in Egypt, Asia, Russia, England,
and don't forget Africa, the motherland.

Tell Antarctica, Australia, North
and South America too,
"If you miss it when it docks,
I feel sorry for you."

This old ship of Zion came my way today.
I ran right to the ship, without delay.

I wasn't unhappy, just glad it came.
Hope when it docks for you, you'll do the same!

LEARN TO BE YOURSELF

If you learn to be yourself, life can be easy-
giving you vision to see.
If you learn to be yourself,
the guidance you learn
comes to you without a fee.

In the years to come, understanding
will bless your heart.
Wisdom is there too, helping to guide
others from the very start.

Summer, Winter, Spring, and Fall-
help us to become fruitful, though we may stall.

It is a stage that we must go through,
approaching problems with hope.
Looking at situations that stand before us,
learning how to cope.

If you learn to be yourself,
love will certainly drop by-
wrapped in a gold package
for that special guy.

Just remember that life can be filled
with enormous wealth.

All you have to do is ...
    LEARN TO BE YOURSELF.

SITTING IN THE PARK

Doing some major thinking, sitting in the park,
children playing - adults walking
until light becomes dark.

Eating at the picnic tables
having lots of fun-
maybe even holding hands,
looking at the afternoon sun.

As the night approaches,
the evening lights come on-
signaling it's time to go home.

Pretty soon the park is deserted,
the place is black dark.
But there's one doing some major thinking,
sitting in the park.

GRAY EYES

There he was standing by the soda shop.
I was staring at him,
my eyes about to pop.

His muscular body,
smooth olive skin and gray eyes-
made me sit still.
My body couldn't rise.

He looked at me with his gorgeous smile
and asked me for my name.
I couldn't remember,
and felt ashamed.

He asked me again
with those smoldering eyes,
suddenly realizing that I was hypnotized.

I said to myself,
"Get a grip girl, speak and don't stutter."
But this sensation that came over me
made me melt like butter.

Butterflies in my stomach, aflutter in my heart-
I knew then that this was love
from the very start.

He pursued me, wooed me-
until I confessed that he was the one for me,
and he was the best.

Eyes sparkling like stars,
his laughter joyful too-
saying, "You are mine.
We are stuck like glue."

My heart pounds whenever I see your face,
bouncing like a ball all over the place.

I was surprised.
We fit just like a glove-
clinging to each other
in everlasting love.

THE LOVE EXPERIENCE

We are looking at each other;
nudeness we don't see-
holding on to each other, you and me.

I'm melting all the time
as you touch my sensitive spots-
crying as you wipe those wet teardrops.

I see the wetness of your face
and wipe your tears as well.
Our bodies are tingling all over the place
more than I wish to tell.

A part of you fits into me like
a key in a lock-or a foot in a sock.

It seems like we are riding on a winding road,
looking for that pot of gold.

Now we are releasing each other-
cuddling and laughing at one another.

We drift off into the land of sleep and slumber
in each other's arms.
I am happy and content with the grace of
your charms.

T.V. SOAP STORY

If ever you are home listening to T.V.,
there seems to be some programs
that are a necessity.

Be aware and know that you can cope
with the adventures of people
on the television soap.

Though we try to give our best,
we are still *the young and the restless*.

Being sure that we don't find too much sorrow,
we go ahead and *search for tomorrow*.

Sometimes becoming *bold and beautiful*
can allow us to get burned,
because we look carefully *as the world turns*.

Thinking our mission is accomplished,
we think that we've arrived,
and we try to protect it all *the days of our lives*.

We practice charity, learning how to give,
because we have only *one life to live*.

THE HURTING TRUTH

There was this story I wanted to tell,
which tells about a life that was set to sail.

About the turmoil, snares, and troubles
that occurred-
and how I overcame them
through prayer and the Word.

I took my time,
in the hope that my siblings would help-
but instead, they're arguing over a petty mess,
as if there is much wealth.

Some of them cursed,
putting other family members in it-
making them a part of lies
that don't fit.

What a terrible, disgusting, mess-
hurting feelings and hearts
that wanted joy and rest.

I pray that God will help in reaching my goal.
He is the one who truly loves me-
mind, body, and soul.

WHO'S THAT LADY?

Did you see the lady standing at the door
with dignity and respect?
Did you see the lady standing at the door
having that staring effect?

She has the career we all want in life -
one with grace and order,
without harsh strife.

She has a walk that is straightforward,
giving her a priceless reward.

She is looking for that special person
to be with always-
to love and honor her, the rest of her days.

I am a lady with dignity and respect,
my world is shared with others.
I am the one to influence my sisters
and my brothers.

I found that special person to be with always.
We shall love, honor, and trust each other
the remainder of our days.

MAN'S HELPER

A woman is a warrior, whatever race she be.
Her beauty, grace, and stature
is there for all to see.

Her nature comes out for the world
with joy unknown or seen.
She seasons the lives around her,
making them glow and gleam.

Her mate looks at her with love,
making him shy to speak.
He says to himself, "This is my helper;
she is mine to keep.

I shall protect her from dangers that appear,
so that she will be with me,
her gentle spirit near."

Blessed is the man who realizes
that though life may go wrong-
he will have a woman to help him along.

If he remembers to love her,
and heed her wisdom every day,
she will have a strong man
to follow all the way.

DANCING IN THE STREET

Calling out to the world to listen
to this jamming beat!
We're getting together, having fun.
We're dancing in the street.

People on the East Coast, West Coast too!
Northerners and Southerners
can come with you.

All that's needed is the music, sweet music,
and it's everywhere you turn.
From slow to fast, and even a little jazz
for each person to learn.

It doesn't matter where you are
just as long as you are there.
Don't take a seat or go to sleep
'cause you'll miss the whole affair.

So, take my hand and follow me.
There are many things to see.
I will guide you to this place
and I won't ask for a fare.

Just be cool, walk beside me,
and I will take you there.

THINKING

Hearing the birds,
watching the swaying of the trees,
makes me thankful that I can enjoy this breeze.

I accept the emotions that flood my mind,
remembering those loved ones
who were beautiful, thoughtful, and kind.

The grassy meadow feels good on my feet,
as I lean on the oak tree taking in the heat.

Beautiful flowers have grown all around
waiting to be picked without a sound.

It would be great if we were immortals, you see.
We could live our lives through eternity.

But alas, we are mortals, on borrowed time.
We get mad at each other and commit a crime.

But I know there is a sweet spirit in this place,
showing me the importance of having grace.

I rise from the oak tree-
walk toward my house,
still hearing birds sing-
with the wind blowing as quiet as a mouse.

Evening has come,
and my emotions are at rest.
I glance at the work that awaits me,
and pledge to do my best.

MR. WINTER

Mr. Winter came by today,
blowing snow, sleet, and frost our way.

He said not a word, just continued a task.
That was his assignment- wearing no mask.

I watched with disgust, and happiness too,
because I could have fun,
but later there would be work to do.

Shoveling snow off the sidewalk,
getting ice off the cars-
hoping not to fall and get any scars.

Perhaps I could get someone to take my place,
so I would be free to join the sled race.

But mom's looking at me with the expression,
"Don't even go there."
Mr. Winter, thanks man. I can't go anywhere.

There is no reply, just the blowing of the wind.
Mr. Winter saying to himself,
"If you don't watch it, I'll do it again."

MISPLACED

I come to this place day by day
feeling belittled, wanting to take a hike,
because there is nothing here for me.
No goal I could really like.

There isn't a path I could truly find,
that enhances the intelligence of my mind.

For those who did not fall between the cracks,
be forever grateful that your life is on track.

I thought things were well,
at least it seemed, but suddenly
my life went down another stream.

Treated like the others
though my maturity level is high.
It's a blow to anyone
who knows the truth and cries.

Maybe I can get away and hopefully I will,
to a place of happiness, where joy is real.

This is not the place for me
to bury my dreams in hurt.
I must get up and go away,
put on a brand new shirt.

MISTREATMENT

Let me tell you about a place
that took away my dignity-
treating me as if I were a child
who had no true identity.

I was used to being able to do as I wanted.
Now I am always watched
like a prisoner being hunted.

Where is my independence I enjoy so dearly?
It's far away from me
and I look for it wearily.

There is nothing like being able
to do your own thing-
not having to ask if you can talk or sing.

It's like you are in childcare or regular school-
reprimanded or suspended
for not following a rule.

Crazy place to be, especially if you are bored.
I must get to a better area
where happiness is stored.

GOING FORWARD

I knew she was there, the dream was real,
standing happily and content,
knowing that her sickness was healed.

I walked closer to her, just to touch her face,
but I couldn't reach her,
because she stood in another place.

I asked her, "Let me stay with you."
But she said,
"No, there are many things you must do."

Sadness came over me
as the tears rolled from my eyes-
feeling hurt as the rain fell from the skies.

I turned around and walked away,
wishing that the night
would turn to day.

We'll be together in the future someday,
talking about our lives on Earth-
as we go our way.

HEY LOVE

Hey love, I would like a word with you.
You seem so distant.
What are you going through?

I know there are bad days
when life isn't so sweet,
but you can make it,
though it might be steep.

Hey love, what does your heart most desire?
Is it success,
hope, or a raging fire?

That burning sensation
that runs through your veins
is only because
you have changed lanes.

Take the time to remember
the great things you have done,
and thank your creator
for things that are to come.

Hey love,
as we walk barefoot on the gritty sandy beach,
remember we have goals to eventually reach.

Those that walk behind us,
we will show them the way-
to be strong, patient, and kind this very day.

Hey love, from this day on
our bodies will come not separate,
but together as one.

We will listen
to the roars of the foamy sea,
looking at the works of our Creator,
you and me.

SNEAKY PEOPLE

Beware of sneaky people,
they have a problem mind.
Beware of sneaky people,
they are very unkind.

Smiling in your face, making an impression,
passing as a friend.
Yet underneath those expressions,
they hate you to the end.

Beware of sneaky people,
trying to help you out with grace-
backstabbing you all over the place.

Beware of sneaky people,
they're good at what they do-
doing things that hurt your spirit
before you ever knew.

Beware of sneaky people,
they can make your life pure hell-
and then express sorrow saying,
"I'm sorry you failed."

Beware of sneaky people,
you see them every day-

but you don't expect the sneaky person
to be someone you loved always.

ANYONE

Can anyone help me?
I need money to live.
Can anyone help me?
I will take just what you give.

Can anyone help me?
There is a project I want to do.
Can anyone help me?
This project could help you.

Can anyone help me? It won't take a lot
of your time.
Can anyone help me?
You'll come out just fine.

Can anyone help me?
My project could soon be complete.
Can anyone help me?
Raise your hand and we'll meet.

Can anyone help me?
Maybe someone will come around.
Can anyone help me?
No one made a sound.

DISCIPLINE

Playing outside, having a good time-
when mother comes to the door,
calling me to come on in.
I want to play some more.

When she goes into the house,
I figured everything was cool.
Yet, I knew I was in hot water
because I broke a rule.

You see, I was supposed to be in the house
before the lights came on.
But I chose to stay outside
and have some more fun.

I'm walking very slowly,
'cause I know what lies ahead soon.
Mom will give me a lecture
and send me to my room.

Well, I'm in the house and Mom's right there.
Dad has a stern look on his face.
I am so afraid now,
'cause I feel out of place.

"Son, who would you like to talk to?
Your mother or me?"
I open my bedroom door saying,
"Mom," with ease.

I'm sitting in my bedroom,
waiting to talk to her, as I always had.
But it isn't her who's in my room.
My dad has come instead.

"Lord, help me." This isn't good-
especially since he walked in with leather.
The tears are rolling down my eyes
because I knew better.

I'm screaming and crying all over the place
as Dad works on my behind.
Afterwards, I always remembered-
kept it on my mind.

I'm outside playing once again
and see the evening lights.
I run to the house.
My mom nowhere in sight.

My dad is sitting in the easy chair reading,
he looks up with a grin.

He says, "My goodness, that boy gets to the house before the others get in."

SPIRITUAL BEING

I walked through a wilderness, no person to see,
except trees, wild animals,
and birds flying over me.

It seemed so strange
as I was trying to reach out,
that no one could see or hear me shout.

Suddenly, someone came before me
with open arms, waiting to hold me-
and do me no harm.

It was a spiritual being
whose face glowed in the night-
gentle and happy that I had come to the light.

I saw people I loved so dearly
who'd left my life years ago-
taking my hand and saying, "Come with us
for there are many people you will know."

I now rejoice with them each day,
no worries or sickness do I see-
for I have become a spiritual being.
This is the life for me.

MONTHS OF THE YEAR

February is running out,
March will be here soon.
April will be spread about-
flowers all in bloom.

May is signaling that summer is coming;
June will be here on time.
July and August will sit there blazing away,
tied up in a bind.

September and October embrace the cool.
November comes and knows,
that December and January are in their place,
with beautiful white snow.

LONELINESS REPLACED

As I travel in darkness, lost and all alone,
I recall the days when life was a joyful song.

The laughter that filled my heart with cheer
gives me no worries-
and no fear.

Exciting people to see or places to go,
watching children playing
and seeing them grow.

The music that is heard has a beat all its own.
It is the sweetest music that I have ever known.

Now the darkness has turned to light,
giving view to the sun,
so beautiful and bright.

The sadness I felt has abandoned me,
happiness stays in my heart,
giving strength and integrity.

I now have a companion,
who is by my side in good times and bad.
No longer am I all alone
and this has made me glad.

A DAUGHTER'S LOVE

I saw her standing by the chair
no word did she speak-
just stared at me, as I screamed out loudly,
my body very weak.

It was my mother-
who I had seen, with her beautiful face.
Brightness beamed all around her,
and happiness filled the place.

The smile she gave was a sign of content,
peace and joy-
for on the other side of her
stood her baby boy.

Then she disappeared from me
and tears came from my eyes.
No one was standing by the chair,
as I stood in awe and surprise.

How could she have been with me
through the trials and tribulations
that have occurred?
Yet far away from me, never saying a word.

But the Lord said to me:

"Why are you sad?
You were together many years,
the best you ever had.
Let her come with me now,
take comfort in knowing
you did your best.
Now she can quietly take her rest.
Cheer up, be strong, fight, and be brave.
We are with you forever
– all the rest of your days."

THE RESPONSIBILITY of FAME

Talented, exceptional,
and beautiful beyond compare.
You are known in the world,
by young and old-
loved everywhere.

Sometimes we don't realize the impact
or worthiness we inspire on the young.
So, there is spiritual unrest,
as if we don't belong.

To satisfy our desire we use dangerous,
materialistic things-
bringing fleeting joy,
but later mars our dreams.

Always be careful of the path you cross,
making sure the successes
will not be a complete loss.

These things are important as we seek
to be known by our names.
Be someone others look up to,
pursuing fortune and fame.

THE WORKPLACE

I disagree with the tactics that happen here.
It can be one-sided when others appear.

The helpers that guide us will sometimes
take a stand.
But otherwise, desert us
when things aren't so grand.

Though you are assigned a place to work
each and every day,
another person that is in charge
may go the other way.

The agreement proposed
by the supervisor who's in charge
can disappear the moment
they are at large.

If this place is to be fair,
one should surely know,
that prejudiced attitudes among some must go.

If there is an issue that must be addressed,
it is one of discomfort and much unrest.

I do hope that in the future
when others come to your place,
employees will treat them with dignity
and grace.

Remember, life comes full circle
and for those you belittle or defame,
it will come back in time
to treat you the same.

MY GUY

I was hoping that seeing you here today,
my life would be with you forever and always.

But in seeing you come I was suddenly shy,
couldn't even look into your beautiful eyes.

Skin was like a chocolate Hershey bar,
shining and sparkling like a bright star.

Body so strong, muscular physique-
Oh my God, that's the type I seek.

A beautiful spirit he carries with him
every time he's near.
I say to myself, "Stay with me, don't disappear."

His smile so warm, teeth glistening white.
Feels so good being with him
in the morning light.

As we walk down the beach barefoot,
laughing out loud-
the others stare at us
because we stand out in the crowd.

THE FOUR SEASONS

Winter makes you shiver,
and you want to keep warm.
So, you get long johns, gloves, caps, clothes,
and coats to cover your arms.

Now it's ready to leave, packing luggage,
on its way home.
Spring came walking in the door
singing a joyful song
and saying, "Come out of those winter clothes
so you can walk along."

Spring stayed for a couple of months,
then decided to go.
Summer came just in time to warm things
and keep them afloat.

Heat is blazing-
and we are getting air conditioners and fans,
playing in a swimming pool, at the beach,
or making sandcastles on land.

Summer stayed,
seeming quite content and at ease.
But Fall came by unexpectedly
and told Summer to leave.

Fall brought his luggage
and decided to paint some colors
of orange, red, yellow, black
and many, many others.

Sweaters, jackets, and long sleeve tops too-
the time is cooler with harvest
and holiday work to do.

As Fall was about ready to go away
it gave us a hint that very day.

Winter was back from his vacation
and rested about a week.
Then it started all over again
with snow so white and deep.

PEOPLE AND ISSUES

There are some people with issues
that cannot be resolved.
They have a sneaky smile on their face
as if not involved.

Yet, know what their motives are
and proceed to avenge,
not knowing the whole story,
just seeking revenge.

There are some people with issues
whose goal is to be unfair-
to those who have desires to get ahead
and show others that they care.

The thoughts that come into their heart
are ones that can't be seen,
because they have an agenda in mind
to back them full steam.

There are some people with issues
who may never experience success-
because they have attitudes toward others
who seek to do their best.

They can hurt themselves in the long run
as they try to hurt others,
who believe in truth and justice
to all sisters and brothers.

Those of you with issues:
try to fix your shame, for when it surfaces
and your true colors are seen,
all will shout out YOUR NAME.

OH, CHILD

Oh child, never be saddened by your plight.
Always remember that God is with you
day and night.

Know that those around you
support you in everything you do.
Be thankful also for a foundation
that makes you feel brand new.

Oh child, never forget the path walked,
never forget your name,
never forget the craft you've made
as you experience fame.

The child that follows behind you
is impressed with your life's achievement.
They tell their friends you are the best
and they listen in agreement.

Oh child, the puzzled look on your face
tells me you don't understand how-
just look further down the road
and you will see happiness right now!

HISTORY OF EQUALITY

A serious problem plagues our history
concerning contributions made by man.
It is the harshness of prejudice
to certain races of the land.

The inventions that made this country great
give homage to some,
but leave the works being used by others
as if it had not been done.

If our history is truly equal,
then invention and works
would be acknowledged small and large
showing the importance of them,
not locked in a garage.

We would know our roots
and others as well,
able to speak about them to strangers
without fail.

So, show the contribution of all races,
young and old,
giving their names and credits
they strongly hold.

Blessings to those who have died,
but whose name goes on.
Blessings to those who live today
as they sing their own song.

Blessings to those in the future,
though we don't know or see their fruits.
Their contributions while a mystery
to our generation,
will be seen in the next group.

A DATE WITH JENNY

"Jenny, would you go out to the movies
with me tonight?
I promise to make you happy
and be a gentleman on sight.

We can go to eat at a place you choose-
order whatever you want.
I will pay for both of us too
and we'll have a lot of fun.

Jenny, I won't have you out all night,
on our first date.
I will do you just right.
You won't be home late."

Jenny thought about this and decided
to go with him,
hoping she wouldn't miss-
and looked at the film.

After the film was over,
she was hungry as could be,
and he took her to the place
she wanted to eat.

When the date was over,
he took her home and it wasn't late.

Jenny felt like a queen on a throne-
saying to herself, "This was great."

They continued to see each other
through their college years-
both were content with each other
knowing their time was near.

So, he says, "Jenny, stay with me
always and forever-
that includes sunny days,
 and stormy weather."

Jenny knew this was true love and her mate,
the one she met on their first date.

He is happy, she is happy-
no more do they seek,
because their joy is a true joy
that they will always keep.

CLASSROOM MEMORIES

Popping gum, putting it under the desk,
or even under your tongue.
If the teacher asks, "Are you chewing?"
You say, "I swear I don't have none."

Eating chips, or pinching off the honey bun
you're having for lunch,
thinking the teacher doesn't have sense enough
to hear that noisy crunch.

Sipping a soda from the vending machine,
spilling a little bit, not very much,
hoping no one saw you
and hurry off in a rush.

Laughing and snickering nonstop while in class,
knowing when the bell rings
the teacher is thinking, "At last."

You remember those crazy days
and think about the teachers you knew-
thankful every day
that they saw success in you.

SCHOOL RULES

I walk up the steps, through the door,
into this boring school.
I hate being in this place
there are too many rules.

You can go to your locker twice a day
to get the books you need.
And if you go another way
you are taken to the principal's office
at full speed.

If you are tardy to your class,
the teacher will ask you, "Why?"
And if the excuse doesn't work,
you get a warning and sigh.

If it happens twice and you say,
"I was in the bathroom stall."
The next thing you have
is early morning study hall.

That means I have to come to school
an hour early,
and if you ask me - that's just plain dirty.

I had a spat with my teacher saying,
"You are wrong!"
Next thing I know, I'm being sent home.

They call my mother-
she is waiting at the door of the house.
I walk in slowly, quiet as a mouse.

Now I've been grounded
until Heaven knows when.
Hoping she doesn't tell Dad-
when he comes in.

She says to me,
"We send you to school to get an education,
and every time I turn around
you have a situation."

Thank goodness, she didn't tell Dad
because I pleaded on my knees.
I promised this wouldn't happen again
so I could feel at ease.

I went back to school two days later
with a new attitude.
I was polite to my teachers
knowing not to be rude.

I make sure I am in class on time
when the tardy bell rings-
take out my assignments among other things.

I am here every day at this place called school.
But I hate going there because
    THERE ARE TOO MANY RULES!

SIDE SHOW EVENT

Step right up!
Get your ticket to see
this one-time show!
There is this lady with two heads-
for everyone to know.

She doesn't bite or touch you,
just likes to be seen.
It won't be that much
and she will be dressed in green.

Oh, you don't believe me?
You think I'm playing around?
Just come on in
and see this and tell all the people in town.

Fifty cents is the charge
and I know that's in your hand,
'cause I saw you get some food
at the refreshment stand.

Come on in!
I see you got the ticket after all.
There she is, wearing the green dress,
bought from the mall.

The people got a seat,
waiting for the show to begin.
The two-headed lady talked to them
then gave a scary grin.

They got scared and ran out of the tent,
going east and west.
Some went north and south as well
to get out of that mess!

The show is over-
and the two-headed lady takes the costume off,
laughing very loudly,
then very softly.

What a terrible thing to do,
but money was the goal we had.
We will do something different next time,
make them happy instead.

PLANTING A SEED

We're sitting by the fire,
talking about ourselves-
what we want for our future,
looking at the books on our shelves.

You have asked me several times
if we could plant a seed.
I am thinking, *now the time.*
So, you can take the lead.

You are taking me upstairs
so that we can shower-
because I know and you know too
that this increases our power.

You have led me to our room,
kissing me all the way,
and I know this is going to be good,
'cause I'm letting you have your way.

We have made it to the bed, and I tell you,
"Please don't stop!"
I am also saying,
"I want to be on top."

"Baby, do whatever you want. I'll just be at ease.
You can ride, have a good time,
as long as you please."

"That's fine with me," I say.
"Let's get started, let me do my thing,
'cause I'm going to ride until you start to sing."

We aren't using protection now,
neither you nor I.
A seed will be planted this very night.

A week or so later I come to you saying,
"We have another mouth to feed."
You are excited, hold me tight and say,
"Baby, we planted that seed!"

LIFE

I thought I knew my basic goal,
but it seems I was mistaken-
because my life went down a path
that left me quite shaken.

How was I to know
that success wasn't my future-
that the courses and degrees pursued
were not so crucial?

The world is at my feet,
the sky is the limit.
A somewhat crazy place to be,
because I could leave any minute.

I have to be careful, for at any time,
things can go away-
then wish it could come back
in that same day.

As I sit and think about these things,
I realize it's my call and I can't quit.
This is my world, mine alone,
so I welcome to it.

CHANGE

Situations come in our lives,
though we try to avoid them-
like flowers picked in spring
leaving just a stem.

Oh yeah, we struggle to do our very best,
and when we do-
so much of it, we finally take a rest.

Life intrigues us every day-
in Winter, Spring, Summer, or Fall.
But we try to make things stay the same-
So, we can know it all.

Some things stay constant in life,
nothing stays the same.
The reality of knowing the paths we walk
shows that everything must change.

There are solutions that come in our heart
so we try to put them in place.
Whatever it is that can make it happen,
we celebrate with grace.

We look at things on a different level,
knowing our goals can change.

So, we come to terms within ourselves
that nothing stays the same.

A NEW WORLD

A beautiful city stands before us,
the grandest of life is there-
no crying, worrying, or despair.
A place where anyone can care.

Sickness, pain, and sadness
lie in the past.
Happiness, joy, shouting, and laughter
are with us at last.

Love is abundant all over the world,
people having fun.
No more darkness showing up,
just the brightly shining sun.

The human race is joined with each other,
all bearing gifts to the King.
His love glows about us
as we stand in unison to sing.

The millennium of a thousand years
starts as the Lord reigns-
teaching lessons that were taught
in the old world, again.

We are shown by the disciples
and prophets with crowns on their heads,
but many of us sit in awe
as we listen to truth, instead.

A beautiful sight with blue skies,
we remember Christ's birth.
And we glorify His holy name,
seeking his love and worth.

Let's go to this land
and worship day by day-
knowing the world is filled with happiness,
forever and always.

LOVE LAND

Come with me, and we'll walk hand in hand,
let me hold you as we talk
and take you to love land.

All the joy that comes our way
brings exciting events to see.
Laughter stays with us all our days,
the reality of sweet peace.

You ask me a question, I don't want to hear,
yet I listen with all my heart.
I will melt and disappear,
'cause the love I have will not part.

The words you say are loud and clear,
"Will you marry me?"
I tell you in a quiet voice, "Yes,"
feeling proud and free.

You put your arms around my waist,
your face held by my hands.
Our feelings magnifying the place
as we go forward to love land.

CRUISING TOGETHER

I went on an ocean cruise,
the sun beaming bright-
stayed on the ship ten days,
dancing and seeing the sights.

While on this cruise,
I met someone who took my heart away.
The sparks that flew
made us mold our thoughts that day.

Meeting each other for dinner,
and later a movie-
cuddled up together, gradually getting sleepy.

Going to our separate rooms
we are both thinking, and know
that when the ship docks,
you will go where I go.

The cruise has come to the end of its journey-
without each other we can't cope.
We say to each other, "Baby, let's elope."

The years have gone by,
our children married finding their way.

We look at each other, smiling to ourselves-
remembering how we eloped that day.

KNOWING MY SAVIOUR

If it wasn't for Jesus, I wouldn't have a friend.
if it wasn't for Jesus,
my life would be a world filled with sin.

But I know He's the son of God,
and His love is my rock.
There is no hasty ticking of a soundless clock.

Who but He can ease my burdens of woe?
It's not me,
because I cannot save my soul.

I climb mountains of grief and horror,
knowing that they are steep-
yet, I go farther.

God is love, this I know,
but sometimes there is doubt in my heart.
But if I trust in His spirit,
nothing will come apart.

I am mindful of my early years
and try to follow those teachings.
Yet sometimes I shed tears
because I am lost in the preaching.

Beneath the cross of Jesus,
all pain would surely die
and be exchanged for prosperity
with a goodness never to hide.

I went through this wilderness
and now I can truly say,
"Praise the lord for giving me strength.
I am saved by mercy and grace."

LESSONS OF LIFE

The last time I saw you,
the world was at your feet.
The rhythm of the music sounded
a good beat.

You had the world before you
with encouragement and fame,
but let it get away from you
leaving sin and shame.

The decisions you made were fruitless,
resulting in tons of carelessness.

It filled your life with mess, having no rest.

Why could you not follow the instructions
given to you each day?
Is it because your mind was stuck
in a cloud of gray?

Yes, I saw you in your ways
and pleaded for you to stop.
But you couldn't see the forest for the trees;
you thought you were on top.

Perhaps if you turn from those wicked ways
great things may come to your door.
Give your best, become stronger,
and your life will soar.

THE ROAD TO SUCCESS

This isn't my life,
I have been misplaced.
I'm going away and must make haste.

My successes and talents that I could show
are left in a hole down below.

I just want to be known to rejuvenate others,
not only my parents, but sisters and brothers.

You want what I want,
but it seems not to come;
perhaps for others,
but not for some.

I want people to know my experiences
with health,
hoping to encourage others to be
positive to themselves.

It's important to be aware
of our place in society-
and I hope I see it
before it slips by me.

I can see the blossoms of the plants in spring,
striving and sprouting and doing their thing.

So why can't I be one of the seasons
telling my story and showing my reasons.

I hope my success comes by the harvest moon
and appreciated very soon.

RISEN

Jesus was sent by His Heavenly Father,
His only begotten son.
He knew there was a price to pay
to save everyone.

Preaching to the multitude,
healing all the sick,
rebuking nasty attitudes,
showing how truth could stick.

Yes, He was seen day by day,
by Christians and sinners alike-
showing them a better vision
of how we must do right.

Told stories or parables to fit our daily lives,
giving them examples of how to live and strive.

Thirty-three years He stayed on this earth,
telling of prophecies unknown.
Some listened carefully,
knowing they weren't alone.

But then one dreadful Thursday night,
soldiers arrested and bounded Him,

knowing that in the morning light
He would be on a cross before them.

Though He preached that on the third day,
He would rise from the dead-
it seemed the people never heard
a word that was said.

He was placed in a new tomb,
being the first to lie there-
rising on the third day
in splendid light everywhere.

The women came to the tomb
and saw that the stone was rolled away.
An angel appeared before them saying,
"He has risen this day!"

They looked in the tomb
and there was only a robe to be found.
Then remembering what He'd said,
they rejoiced in joyful sound.

Hallelujah to the lamb of God,
our Lord He will always be.
Blessed is the entire world-
this day He has given us victory.

EASTER CELEBRATION

Easter baskets, Easter hats,
Easter shoes and socks.
Easter bunny, Easter candy and eggs to stock.

It only comes but once a year
so the outfits we have won't fade.
We model them down 5th Avenue
in the New York Easter Parade.

The excitement we have just won't stop,
as cars roll down the street.
There are so many things to do, people to see.

I can't wait to go to the mall
and find my Easter dress-
watch people stare me down,
as I look my Sunday best.

The celebration has died down, eventide sets in.
Easter is over and has left us once again.

But colored eggs are left here,
cakes and candies so sweet.
We can all settle down and enjoy
our Easter treats.

A MIGHTY LOVE

When a person truly loves you,
they will go that extra mile-
and because they enjoy your company,
they will stay and sit a while.

What is our future destiny
if we don't consider their pain?
There may be a price to pay
for our ruthless vain.

When a person truly loves you,
and needs you by their side-
always be quick to assist them,
for they will know you tried.

In those dark days
when you feel there is no hope,
true devotion to each other
helps you both to cope.

A mighty love can sustain
your knowledge and ability.
A mighty love can conquer
all of your humility.

When a person truly loves you,
they will forever be in your midst-
for there is no truer love
than a love you can't dismiss.

LONELY NIGHT

I'm walking home once again at night
with the stars.
And it's because there is no cab-
nor is there a car.

There is no one on the street;
danger may lie ahead.
Because I didn't communicate or listen
to what was said.

Finally, I'm walking through the gate,
unlocking the door of my house.
There are no children.
Not even a spouse.

I just live here by myself,
no one do I expect-
except for maybe a computer
or a television set.

It's so boring in this place,
there is no one to call.
The person I like talking to
isn't answering at all.

I can't wait to get to work
and talk to the people there.
Maybe I can meet someone
who understands and cares.

Until that time, I'll go to bed
and sleep away the night-
wake up in the morning
to sun so nice and bright.

I'm at work,
but night will be coming very soon.
And I will be walking alone again,
with no one but the stars and moon.

THE TUB

What is all this washing about?
I do it all the time.
I know I don't smell,
and my clothes look fine.

Okay, so there's a spot on my pants,
and I've been playing in dirt.
That ain't nothing
but a few specks on my shirt.

My hands are a little sticky,
and my nails are filled with mud-
but that doesn't mean I have to get in the tub.

I made three home runs playing baseball today.
A little dirt was on my shirt, socks, and shoes
-anyway.

I'm coming into the house
and hear water running fast.
It's from the bathroom.
Mother talking at full blast.

I don't understand why she is so upset-
but there are footprints on the floor,
where she just swept.

I look at myself in the mirror
and see I need a couple of rubs.
Mother is looking and telling me to
"Get in the tub!"

Well, I'm getting out now-
clean, I'm sure for years.
But Mom comes and looks me over saying,
"YOU DIDN'T GET BEHIND YOUR EARS!"

DINNER TROUBLE

Coming to the table for a great feast-
meatloaf waiting on the table as I take my seat.

Vegetables are English peas,
mashed potatoes too.
Cornbread is there to help us get through.

I get everything on my plate
except those English peas,
hating them with a passion-
though Mom puts them on with ease.

She says, "If you eat five English peas,
then you can get up and go-
when the others leave."

Frowning, I sit there looking very mad,
hoping if I pout enough-
she'll let me go instead.

I'm forcing them down one by one,
tears flowing from my eyes-
as I try to eat those things I despise.

Now I have the last one in my mouth,
swallowing it with relief-

Visions of Life

I can't wait to get away from all that grief.

Dessert is on the table now,
peach cobbler and ice cream.
I'm running to the kitchen now,
the first to be seen.

It's served on paper plates,
and I'm ready to eat!
Since I ate my veggies - including the peas,
dessert is truly a treat.

OBSERVING REALITY

Grief and happiness,
unfairness and just-
can make our world of understanding
an extreme must.

We climb mountains,
walk on rocky roads, tip toe on ice-
knowing that if we miss one beat
it won't be something nice.

But that is the way of our world today.
Our feelings in our hearts-
go the other way.

If only we could accept life as it stands,
then we can ask others to serve
the poor in the land.

Maybe in years to come
we can learn to give.
That would be a plus-
to see the light and live.

A FAMILY OF NINE

There once was a couple
who produced a family of nine.
They believed with guidance
things would be fine.

As each child left,
going into the world to pursue success-
the others in the family saw them do their best.

But when troubles and trials emerged
on the scene-
they lost their ways in leadership
and vision so keen.

The couple hoped the children
could stick together and stand-
together through precious times
and stormy weather as family can.

When time came
for the couple to go live with their Lord,
they hoped all would stand in one accord.

But somewhere along the way,
the foundation went wrong.

Hazy fog and unsteadiness came-
among them all.

Happiness, joy, and unity
was what they wanted back-
by getting connected to each other,
they got themselves on track.

The couple watched and rejoiced with hope,
pleased with their family of nine.
For the children were together again,
and life would be just fine.

SADDEN THOUGHTS

I'm tired of being alone, with no route to take.
No money do I have, and none to make.

The talents that I have get me no job to work.
It makes me very angry-
when others look and smirk.

There was a time in my life
when my world was colorful and exciting!
Now I sit and continuously do a lot of writing.

My family despises who I am,
some curse me in disrespect-
and I think about this saying,
"There is no love to accept."

How can I be alone, and have something to give,
showing ideas about ways to live?

In my life I want all to know
that life gives us lessons
on how we should grow.

PICNIC FUN

Let's go to the park and have a picnic.
Play a game or two.
We will meet you at pavilion four
while the sky is still blue.

You buy the drinks and get forks and knives.
I'll buy the food, and get music-
that's jamming live.

There are fun games that we can play:
horseshoes, frisbee, or dance all day.

This event will be something all of us can see.
A jolly good time is what this will be.

Don't be unsure, or sing a sad song-
just remember that we all belong.

Go up and down on the seesaw,
swing high on the swings.
Don't forget the merry-go-round
and all the joy it brings.

The sun is going down,
darkness will come with the moon.
But we will picnic once again - real soon.

SPRING SEASON

It's a mystery of how plants can grow,
sometimes fast or very slow.

But when the season of spring comes about,
it makes people want to dance, run, and shout.

The warm weather is a sign of events to come,
and we rejoice with all or maybe some.

Flowers blossom, along with the trees,
we sit and praise God for fulfilling our needs.

We think on these things,
looking around-
happy to hear birds sing.

These are some things we see when it's time.
Costing us no fee-
not even a dime.

EXPRESSIONS OF SORROW

Sorrow has come into your place
making it hard to accept-
a person loved with all your heart
took another step.

Left alone, by yourself,
the event has broken your heart.
And there comes this feeling within you
that makes you fall apart.

But always remember the world goes on-
pray for strength and courage.
You can make it if you try.
Don't put your life in storage.

There are many things the Lord has
in store for you.
Just understand the path
and become brand new.

Feel comfort knowing
that they're at peace this day,
and spiritually they will take you forward,
guiding all the way.

MONEY

What is this thing called money?

"I gotta have it," some people say.
"It makes me feel happy all day."

This piece of paper is always used.
It can be a good thing, or greatly abused.

Helpful in dealing with great hunger,
it may be an aid for sleep and slumber.

Some call it pure gold, others say dollars,
or one could become a great scholar.

Some want a vacation
to places that are hot and sunny.
But in order to get there - it takes money.

Most times when it's needed,
you have to get a job.
And some who've had it always-
could be a snob.

Don't forget the inheritance,
or the trust fund for Johnny.
When he turns 21, that's his MONEY, HONEY!

PRECIOUS GEM

They disappeared at the blow of the wind,
but a gift was left to me.
All I needed was to treat it
like a precious gem on my tree.

There came a time in my life
when money disappeared,
and I had to sell that gem
to someone I hated and feared.

The funny part about it was that they had
other gems and more-
saw the little that I had
and took it for them to store.

I eventually gave up everything,
being pressured and despised-
ending up in a homeless place
while tears dropped from my eyes.

What did I do that was so wrong-
that my siblings would hurt me this way?
Perhaps they were afraid of the money
I'd receive-and *that* would not be okay.

THE ONE I LOVE

There are many things I do with the one I love,
so much to say-
talking about our lives together,
helping each other each day.

Walking in the rain with the one I love
makes some problems better.
It can be a soothing thing,
allowing us to be together.

Talking on the phone with the one I love
gives me time to think-
watching the paths of our future,
hoping those goals won't sink.

Going to church with the one I love
gives me a joy unknown.
And the principles that we learn
will forever be our own.

Marrying the one I love
makes me feel so fine.
Leveling those bumpy places-
leaving our troubles behind.

Having a family with the one I love
makes me feel so grand.
And we relish those glorious days
as we walk hand in hand.

FUN ON THE BEACH

Let's go crazy, let's have fun,
walking on the sandy beach
in the golden sun.

We'll build castles in the sand,
show the latest moves and latest dance.

There's plenty laughter, shouting too-
learning more actions that we can do.

We'll go swimming, the surf in one,
riding those foamy waves until we are done.

Play some games that require us to think,
while others make us sweat
to the point of wanting a cold drink.

Who can win and put their friends to shame?
Only those who get the concept,
knowing the purpose of the game.

We could stay here all day long,
playing cards and singing songs.

Some just hum not knowing the words,
while others snicker thinking that's absurd.

It's time to go, night is here.
The sun is done. Now it disappears.

We wave good-bye to our friends,
knowing our fun has come to an end.

See ya tomorrow.
Same time.
Same place.
And go our different ways-
with a glowing face.

CHECKING IT OUT

Sun dress looking good on me-
sitting under the tree with a windy breeze.

Eating food, drinking pop, my friend and I.
We catch each other's expressions
with our eyes.

Smiling very shyly as he talks about his day
and hoping not to stare at his eyes - so gray.

They seem to change colors when he is calm.
They're light brown or green as a leafy palm.

We are listening to music as I sway and groove-
watching as my body moves.

Feeling so good as my back is turned,
I know he's saying to himself, "Burn baby burn."

He has on the sexiest shirt and shorts.
Kaki in color - with style, of course.

I am five-six, and he is six-three-
I consider that a giant over me.

To me, he is not perfect,
yet there are faults to be found.
Just like me.
we can still be bound.

So, as we converse,
I think dreamingly and sigh,
we belong together-
he and I.

FEAR TO HOPE

I looked at the road,
as I thought about the years
when all was delightful-
no shedding of tears.

I needed someone to hold me tight.
But no one was visible to calm me that night.

It was a strange darkness that came over me.
I struggled with my mind to get clarity.

What is this thing that has come to my heart?
It was a frightening thought from the very start.

Shaking with emotion, I was scared to no end-
thinking about how this ever began.

But as I prayed for security
my world was left behind.
Being in the arms of my Heavenly Father
came a peace I could surely find.

Now I have the serenity to trust God-
day by day,
and I glorify His name forever, always.

CHILDHOOD SWEETHEART

Had a childhood sweetheart.
Quen was his name.
He sat in front of me in class,
and my life was never the same.

I noted every speck of his body
from the top of his head-
to the bottom of his feet.
Everything about it was clean and neat.

I knew this must be love,
because all I can think about was him-
but schoolwork should be my first priority.
Success must not be dimmed.

I giggled when he talks to me-
because I was so shy.
He smiled and winked at me
out of the corner of his eye.

Asked me for my phone number,
couldn't remember what it was.
But it finally came to me-
so he could give me a buzz.

My telephone rang that same night
and he identified himself.
I listened to him as I put books on the shelf.

Man, I couldn't believe myself
for my tongue was tied like a rope.
But I got myself together-
crossing my fingers with hope.

The senior prom dance came around
and Quen asked me to be his date.
He picked me up, gave me a rose, saying
"You look great!"

Everyone who saw us said,
"You guys look good together!"
Later, Quen held me even tighter
in the cool night weather.

After eating breakfast,
we drove around looking at the sights.
I arrived home with a glow
at the dawn's early light.

We both had a good time
and talked about future events.
Graduation was around the corner
and invitations had been sent.

As we marched down the aisle
to receive our diplomas with proud faces,
I thought about the life we would live
in far-away places.

We talked with each other
and said we must never be apart.
I told him quietly,
"Quen, you are my childhood sweetheart!"

TAKE IT AS IT COMES

There are places you don't want to go,
because work is not fast but very slow.

Coming every day is quite a chore.
You want to get away forevermore.

There are many roads people have
for you to follow-
hoping to see a better tomorrow.

Each day is taxing on your body completely.
Sometimes you don't care
if it's not done neatly.

You have good days and bad-
making you happy or sad.

That's why in life we take it as it comes,
hoping it soon to be over-
knowing and wishing for that day
on a 4-leaf clover.

THE FEEL OF INSTRUMENTS I LOVE

I'd love to hear a saxophone,
an instrument of my heart-
to blow and take me to the place
I lived from the very start.

But then, a piano and xylophone
can make chills run down my spine,
and I count the half or whole notes
as they give a rhythm-
that makes me feel so fine.

 Sometimes a harmonica or the drums
can remind me of the jungle
and I dance a dance so wild
that others feel I may stumble.

A violin can soothe me
when I feel the world on my shoulder.
Then make me holler
because I have become bolder.

The instruments have a rhythm that play
different tones - and that's okay with me.
The best refreshing thing to have-
when you want no company.

THE VOYAGE OF TIME

Time has been for us or against us.
It all depends on the expectations that come
in our lives.

Sometimes we have loved ones
who depart from us spiritually.
It was their time.
For us a time of sorrow, for we miss them
at the moment of their demise.

The time of happiness comes the moment
a child sets foot on this earth.

We rejoice and give thanks to God-
for the child's safety.

There is a time to work, for we must support
our families and give hope to those in need.

Then comes a time to plant food
that will be harvested in the season of Fall.
But the crops may be ruined by disasters.

This is a time of distress.
It hurts those who depend on that food
for the hungry.

Time can be blessed through the union of two people. It can bring about a better relationship from both sides of a family.

Time is saddened when divorce or separation happens.
We live with the hope of reconciliation,
ironing out problems through discussion.

Time brings about wisdom to all and we teach it to those of the present.
As we acknowledge our past,
looking at technology that is unknown
to our life-
but a part of the future.

FATHER TYPES

There are many types of fathers
who take you under their wing.
Some give you instructions
on how to make or fix things.

A father can be an instructor, pastor, or friend;
and congratulate you on awards you win.

We envy some who have had successful lives;
rejoice with others
who may not even have the drive.

Fathers can even be your brothers,
who show you a way to do schoolwork
you don't understand-
show different methods of becoming a man.

They can be strong or very weak,
but still give love you can continuously keep.

It is said by many people
that a man isn't supposed to cry,
but fathers are people too.
Why should their emotions be dry?

Fathers become an example to their sons,
when they have their own businesses to run.

They teach children dignity in being truthful
to themselves each day.
And with that all learn about the world
when sad or happy always.

The best father of all is the Heavenly Father
who made all things completely.
We as humans have a tendency to forget,
so we take and possess things greedily.

OH, YE OF LITTLE FAITH

The world and I had lost our way-
a voice of song said to me, "Oh, ye of little faith."

I was led to a place unknown to me,
where only nature could be seen-
and I know it was His and His alone
in many colors and shades of green.

He asked, "Are you responsible for these things
that stand before you?
Can you throw lightning or have a sky so blue?

These animals that are seen,
You named them one by one-
and tamed them every day,
in the blazing sun.

But did you create them
and supply all their needs?
They have no doubts,
and allow Me to lead.

If you have just a little faith
as a grain of mustard seed,
you could say to a mountain,
Step aside and leave.

Nothing would be impossible for others or you,
through faith and loyalty-
all would be true.

Oh, ye of little faith,
always remember and know
that I have the final answers
as you continue to grow."

ENCOURAGEMENT

I detect there is something wrong,
and don't know what.
Do you think you don't belong,
and must stay in this rut?

I truly understand the problems you may face-
for there is turmoil and backstabbing,
all over the place.

What is your dream or what is your will?
Can you let out the steam and stay quite still?

I see this every day; I'm sure you do too.
We have many associates,
but our friends are few.

Be brave and spiritual-
stay humble and full of cheer.
Know you are safe,
with nothing to fear.

VAN RIDE

Pickup is around 6:40 am - honking is its sound.
No one else is waiting; none stands around.

Darkness is upon us, though light is on its way-
giving to a better morning and a better day.

It's driven by our driver; the route is his own.
Sometimes by another, whose face is unknown.
Others need no assistance; they do for
themselves.

There are some vans that prohibit chewing
gum, eating, and drinking can't be done.
It can remind you of school rules- that's no fun.

Pick up time for going home is 2:55 pm or more.
Some wait for their own ride,
to get things done at the store.

Some get home at 3 pm, others by 4 or later -
depending on how many are there,
whichever is greater.

Now the van is at my house.
In the morning I'll stand-
waiting for my ride in the big white van.

MOTHER'S GIFT FROM GOD

M Maturity bringing a child into the world

O Observant of all the girls and boys

T Timely with things that are important to do

H Hopeful for blessings of joy that may help you

E Examples of integrity, firmness, and discipline when needed

R Reality she teaches about life and rules we must heed

The words that are written represent the
mothers who turn the hands of time.
It is a truth for all to see-
though it might put us in a bind.

God gave us mothers-
so that her love could bring us together,
and teach us the importance
of obeying His word that we can live forever.

TO A PHENOMENAL MOTHER

She is there when you are sad and down-
happiness she brings when there are frowns.

Her wisdom and thoughts give encouragement
to the young and old.
It's a standing foundation-
filled with love untold.

She is solid all the way - very understanding.
But can sometimes be quite demanding.

She gets up inspiring others to be leaders
in later years.
Listens to our troubles,
when we break down in tears.

Rocks her baby singing lullabies
that soothe the soul.
Quietly lulling them to sleep-
dreaming of sweet cinnamon rolls.

Knows her children, their thoughts,
character, and ways-
Can pinpoint who did what,
though no one says.

Helping her mate to create a home of warmth.
Daily in their lives-
steadfast, immovable by his side.

Taking her baby to kindergarten,
hearing it cry and scream-
wanting to get the child as her tears flow
like a stream.

Happy to see her child at the end of the day,
hugging it tightly without delay.

She cooks, sews, and mediates
when necessary to do.
A lady of refinement.
A phenomenal mother, so true.

These duties continue from dusk to dawn,
with no complaint, no not one.

What a wonderful gift God gave to this world.
Her presence brings passion with open arms-
filling life with her love, wisdom, and charm.

SUCCESS

How many hills do we climb to make ourselves
a success?

For some, it is at the first door that opens,
and it falls in their lap.

Others walk through several doors and then
there is a block we must tear down in order to
open it.

Sometimes we go down a road that seems safe
as we go forward. Then we realize that there is
danger in our midst, causing us to run back,
to revamp our thoughts.

We start again on the road to success-
like the darkness of the earth and the
brightness of the sun.
It comes in many forms and fashions.

Know who you are and what you can do.
And when the time is right-
all will see the best of you.

It is at that time that your success is known to the
people.

BECOMING A YOUNG ADULT

When we were children,
our worries were small.
We would talk with each other and have a ball.

But as the years passed and life became real,
our roles suddenly changed-
as we put up a shield.

Whispers in the dark,
sounds unknown to our ears-
make us sometimes wonder
about the later years.

The foundation laid is a concrete beginning,
and as we become adults-
we want to continue winning.

We want to keep a path that's clear,
no obstacles in our way-
makes our lives easier, day by day.

As we grow old and grow in wisdom,
it's important to be firm in our beliefs-
knowing the experiences we have had
may spare others that same grief.

Get yourself together,
acknowledge your faults-
be willing to succumb to fate.

For if we learn to do these things-
our reality will not turn to hate.

MOTHER'S SPIRITUAL GUIDANCE

A mother's spiritual guidance comes from God,
sometimes it's understood or quite odd.

We are mystified by its presence
taken out of place.
Wondering what will come next
with a strange look on our face.

She can talk with us quietly without a big fuss,
Making us aware of our surroundings-
as we learn to trust.

I can feel her spirit,
when tears flow from my eyes.
Knowing that I am filled with sadness,
no comforting sounds do I hide.

Though her spirit is with me day by day,
I'd like to touch her humanly-
to take the pain away.

But that's not the way of life,
so we take it with a grain of salt.
There is no one to blame-
or at fault.

Since we have no control over the spiritual
world, God has graced us with memories-
so sweet.
We think of Mother's spiritual values,
and take them to the street.

BITTERNESS WITHOUT A CAUSE

What happens to people
when greed covers their mind?
They seem to become ruthless,
one of a kind.

We see it each day with their cruel,
wicked ways,
and wonder sometimes if there
is happiness any day.

The bitterness in their hearts flowing
through a small hole.
It lingers, thriving on the madness of old.

Stealing fun-filled ideas, making it ugly to see.
Praying for failure for all humanity.

How terrible to possess a character like that,
never realizing the turmoil-
and results of this act.

Perhaps someday we will learn
to be respectful to each other,
and be at peace with one another.

BEING AN EXAMPLE

It takes a lot of good timing, a lot of good love
to live and fly with grace,
like a white turtle dove.

A foundation so powerful
that confidence is shown-
knowing for sure, that you're not alone.

Picking up the pieces which life has scattered
in the world before us,
gluing it together slowly
without having a big fuss.

I know this is important,
being an example to the young,
for there is peace in understanding
where paths have begun.

Children behind us are watching
what we do or say,
Seeing if we can practice what we preach
all the way.

If we can be ourselves,
letting our conscience be the guide,
All can be well, nothing must we hide.

Tell of your accomplishments,
an ability to trust as you teach.
It will be an inspiration-
and for the stars they will reach.

FULFILING OUR LIVES

Paths that are walked, are the lanes we cross,
filled either with riches or unseen loss.

But we understand-
and know our various shapes,
before we are bound by wads of tape.

Listening to a rhythm of the falling rain,
gives us a beat to the accomplishments we gain.

The quietness of Winter,
the brightness of Spring,
is summer fun-
as we hear the birds sing.

We take our cues from lessons learned,
enjoying the profits produced and earned.

Whether we are greater than great
or lesser than less,
we must cross the lanes together
and do our best.

VIOLENCE

Violence seems to rock our world-
even when we try to stop it.

It's not our call,
the source is bigger than we know.

Yet, for some reason humanity feels
they have it all under control.

They will work on a case until it runs cold,
but forever wonder if there was one piece
of evidence that was overlooked.

Some cases are never solved-
even when there is possible connection to it.

It is remarkable that some crimes puzzle man
two to three centuries after committed.

There seems to be no answers.
We are forever looking for clues, DNA,
fingerprints, it causes one to be uneasy,

But in the end,
the violence still prevails in the world.

We are carnal humans, not God.
Only He has the answer.
We are just waiting and listening for a call.

PROBLEMS

I got major problems that stand around me.
Not on legs, just emotions;
sometimes visible to the eyes sightless.

Perhaps the voice strains signs of displeasure.

Nevertheless, they flow in a continuous cycle.
I can't seem to solve the situations that are
before me.

It's puzzling. Won't leave.
Seems to come in different forms and fashions.

You think it's nipped in the bud,
but something else pops up.

I guess that's the way of the world
as it revolves around the sun.
Same stuff, 365 days of the year.

There has to be some joy somewhere out there.
Hope I can be happy anyway.

This *ain't* heaven,
it's HELL ON EARTH!

AUTHORITY

Authority is important in our lives.
It brings about control when there is havoc.
The problem with it is that sometimes we get it twisted.

Why does it happen?

Perhaps some feel that to be noticed, they must be seen.

All know that a power has been given and one would hope to be humble or thankful that they were graced with that position.

If it is abused in any type of way, we will pay one way or the other.

For we can be downgraded, demoted from a position, even despised by your employees.

Loneliness is your partner when associates should be there.

Authority comes in many forms: teacher, preachers, parents, employers, CEO's.

Though these people are in position, they answer to someone higher.

Maybe the city, state, or federal government, and finally, the president, who must guide and listen to the concerns of all people whether rich or poor.

This is not a dictatorship. People can vote you in or out. Let us be careful and understand that we are all human and nobody or nothing is everlasting.

THE CONTROL FACTOR

People are afraid of some things that exit the norm. Yet, want to be a part of the action when that norm turns out to be a successful avenue.

Why is the fear of failing a project so devastating?

Is it because we have no faith in ourselves?

All have fallen short because of the sins that we bear.

Can we not confess our wrong without denying the principles of good?

We have a commitment to the world to do our best, be an example, knowing that in the end,

God has it all under control.

ANGER

What is the purpose of being angry?
Does it solve the problem that stands before us?
Revenge can cause lives to be shortened.

It's a bitterness we can live without.
Why despise a person with your anger that kills
a soul? A soul that produces peace with
understanding.

Life ain't easy with its turmoil and problems.
We should go forward, pick up the pieces that
have scattered during our rough periods.

When do we dispose of the anger that has
drenched the roads of unhappiness?
Does it not make it hard to look clearly at
ourselves?

It's present in our body language how we feel
about others. We must learn to conquer this
feeling and think positive as obstacles come
before us.

It's a journey we must all take to better
ourselves. If we just learn to pace ourselves,
the anger we possess might just disappear.

There is a place for you, for us, for this world. All we have to do is smile, filling our hearts with a tenderness knowing that in the end joy is our foundation.

Our mission is accomplished.

EXAMPLES DADS POSSESS

Dad, you are a solid rock in our lives, glued to the principles you've learned.

It's a remarkable feeling to know that though we all have our ways, you will negotiate a possible compromise that can make each of your children happy.

As a husband and mate, you support your wife in all of her endeavors, no matter how much of your time it takes.

Back in the days when your children were young, you gave some rules that were never to be crossed, yet we would try you anyway.

The consequences behind them were either physical or of firm rebuke.

There are times when your daughters can wrap your hearts, melting it from hard to soft.

Your sons look to you as an example of integrity, hope, passion, and guidance. Teaching them how to fish, showing them parts needed to work through manpower.

In the end, we are proud to acknowledge you as a leader with leadership qualities.

"HAPPY FATHER'S DAY"

SPIRITUAL AND EARTHLY FATHERS

I have a spiritual Father, an earthly one too.
They counsel me in my life-
whatever I strive to do.

My earthly father I can see,
touch him physically with my hand.
My spiritual Father I cannot see,
but bids me join the Christian band.

The Spiritual Father never dies,
He's always there for us.
But the earthly father has limited time,
so his instructions require us to trust.

I am blessed in this world
to be given a choice on how I want to learn.
And in this way,
I see examples of how to not get burned.

My spiritual Father sends an angel,
when I stray or get off track.
Then guides me in another direction-
cutting me some slack.

The earthly father that I see
can make mistakes in his life.
Yet knows that he tried to do his best,
though there may be strife.

When they work together (spiritually and
physically), it becomes a special bond we know.
It's the best thing for all of us to have,
a love that continues to grow.

LIFE CHALLENGES

You want everyone to like your ideas,
but each person has their own opinion.
Some believe in you, others despise you
and the image brought before them.

The questions put before you seem easy,
yet the answers given are criticized as petty-
childish, unthinkable, a disgrace to society.

What is the purpose of being productive if your
associates have made a pact - to strike down
any ideas you present to them?

Disrespect is your agenda. No thoughts of
dignity cross your line.

No matter how brilliant you are, you're still
under a microscope, and if anything messes up-
the responsibility hits you.

Even those who know the cause say nothing.
They sit easy and watch the episode with a sigh
of relief, after all, it's clear with them.

Some snicker, even laugh loudly at the one in
charge.

Do we think about the consequences behind these things?

Be careful of your smirks, defiance, and evil ways.
It could BACKFIRE on you for LIFE.

MANKIND

Each day presents a different subject for all to see. Some can be easy, others difficult, but that's life.

We come from an angle of worry and despair yet understand that it's not any fault of mine or others who abide in this place.

What comes before us may be a difficult situation to solve, but we try to work it anyway.

We are human, our thoughts are of mortal decent, forgetting that there are some things that only our Lord can do.

The diseases and germs we carry float our environment regularly, but we work and present solutions that are beneficial to us and our planet.

God puts man in charge letting them make choices about our spiritual beings.

Hoping we will teach the children truth, love, and happiness. Justice, in our lives, completes our world for all mankind.

CONCLUSION

I am the youngest of my siblings. Their ages range between seven and nineteen years older than I. Needless to say, I had a wide variety of antics to witness and enjoy. The character and humorous ways of my siblings captured and held my attention.

Writing brought back memories I did not realize I could recall.

In some ways, it was as if I was transformed back to happier times when my mother was still alive.

As I continued to write, I found myself healing pieces of me that were threatening to leave with her. I realized there was much life left for me to live.

In writing this book, I understand and hope that you find this to be true too: Life is painful at times, but there is also joy. It is a vicious cycle, but one that is rewarding if only you dare to believe.

About the Author

Helen Teryce "Teri" Jeffries is a native of Little Rock, Arkansas. She is a graduate of Little Rock Central High School and Philander Smith College with a B.S. Degree in Mathematics.

In her spare time, the author enjoys reading, writing, and the arts.

The first-time author resides in Maumelle, Arkansas.

"I can see the blossoms of the plants in spring, striving and sprouting to do their thing."

-Helen T. Jeffries

Thank you

www.ingramcontent.com/pod-product-compliance
Lightning Source LLC
Chambersburg PA
CBHW072017110526
44592CB00012B/1338